EURO - HAIKU

First published 2007 by IRON Press
5 Marden Terrace, Cullercoats, North Shields,
Northumberland, NE30 4PD, England
tel/fax: +44 (0) 191 253 1901
email: ironpress@blueyonder.co.uk
www.ironpress.co.uk

ISBN 978-0-9552450-2-2

Typeset in Garamond CE 11 pt

Printed by Aeroprinting Ltd., Jarrow-on-Tyne

IRON Press is a member of Independent Northern Publishers

IRON Press books are distributed by Central Books
and represented by Inpress Ltd, Northumberland House,
11 The Pavement, Pope's Lane, Ealing, London W5 4NG,
Tel: +44 (0)20 8832 7464, Fax: +44 (0)20 8832 7465
email: stephanie@inpressbooks.co.uk
www.inpressbooks.co.uk

EURO - HAIKU

A Bi-Lingual Anthology

Edited and introduced by David Cobb

Contents

We acknowledge publication of Emmanuel Lochac's monostich in *Emmanuel Lochac: ses visages et leurs énigmes,* by Jacques Arnold, pub. La Jointée, Paris, 1994; Dag Hammarskjöld's haiku in *En orörd sträng,* by Kaj Falkman, pub. Ordfront förlag, Stockholm, 2005; and the haiku by George Seferis is an extract from *Sixteen Haiku* taken from *George Seferis: Complete Poems* tr. Edmund Keeley and Philip Sherrard, pub. Anvil Press Poetry, 1995.

Most of the English translations in this anthology are the collaborative work of the author with the editor, David Cobb, sometimes entirely the author's own work, sometimes entirely the editor's, but we gratefully acknowledge the following exceptions:

Juan Cervera, *tr. George Swede and Anita Krumins;*
Mirsad Denjo, *tr. Gordana Valand;*
Georges Friedenkraft, *tr. Brian Fergusson;*
Dag Hammarskjöld, *tr. Kaj Falkman;*
Alain Kervern, *tr. Janet Ormrod;*
Zoe Savina, *tr. Matina Spetsiotis and Aghapi Daifa;*
George Seferis, *tr. Edmund Keeley and Philip Sherrard;*
Dimitar Stefanov, *tr. Angelina Christanova;*
Tomas Tranströmer, *tr. Graham High and Gunvor Edwards;*
Alenka Zorman, *herself with Alan McConnell Duff.*

David Cobb

SINCE founding the British Haiku Society in 1990, David Cobb has edited six anthologies for the Society, three for IRON Press, and one for the British Museum. His personal collections of haiku and haibun are plentiful and include bilingual editions (Dutch, German, and Slovene); details on his website, http://davidcobb.members.beeb.net/index.html. Prizes include the *Cardiff International Haiku Prize* (1991), the *Takahama Kyoshi Prize* (2006), the *Sasakawa Award* for an almanac of English seasonal images (2004), and *Haiku Society of America Merit Book Awards*. Cobb's haiku and haibun are often set in his beloved East Anglia, where he writes English lessons for schools in Africa, the Arab World, and the Far East.

Foreword

IN 1992 IRON Press brought out *The Haiku Hundred* — a hundred haiku by eighty-one English-speaking haiku poets, from both sides of the Atlantic. The success of this starter encourages us to offer an even more exotic dish.

Now the ingredients come from no fewer than twenty-six countries, for in the interim haiku has become poetic fare enjoyed throughout Europe. Not only does it seem that there is no country without writers of haiku, there are already a number of countries where they have formed a society to share and discuss work and engage in related activities. This was made abundantly clear at the inaugural European Haiku Congress, held in Bad Nauheim, Germany, in May 2005. (See *Links* at end.)

Haiku from Britain are read all over Europe and frequently translated. Now, in this anthology, you can see the flow from the other side of the sluice.

Just eighty haiku? A mere drop from *la mer, il mare, das Meer,* the ocean of possibly a million haiku that have been published in Europe during the past fifteen years or so. But eighty haiku can make an impact, give a nudge to the soul, that eight hundred or eight thousand haiku would diffuse. *Multum in parva,* as they claim in Rutland. To have gone in search of the 'eighty best' haiku would have been futile; the aim was less fraught, to put together a book the reader might want to return to, always finding new layers of meaning and emotion. Variety of form, content and mood were also desirable, even if some of the poems might neglect principles that delight the heart of the haiku purist. That includes, of course, the half dozen 'found' haiku, lines taken from longer poems.

The 'found' poem is still a red rag to some people, but not to the British scholar R H Blyth (1898-1964), whose writings have done so much to promote the understanding and the writing of haiku, not only in English-speaking countries, but throughout Europe. We believe it adds spice and perspective to this collection when we include a few 'found' haiku by poets living long before haiku had become a familiar genre in the West. This might suggest that the predisposition to write something like haiku (a relish, as Tony Conran reminds us, for 'slenderness, tenderness', and above all 'loneliness — the loneliness of detachment, not the bitter isolation of frustrated desire') has been latent in our continent for much longer than haiku have actually been written here.

Wherever you look in Europe there are variations in the form and style in which haiku may be written. On the one hand we find the 'strict form', in 5-7-5 syllables, a requirement innately suited to the Japanese language, but never set in stone there, and unsuited to become a universal rule. There is not space here to explain why this 'rule' may cause problems in most if not all European languages, though some languages, and some writers, may be more comfortable than others with it. On the other hand we have 'free form', with no rigid syllable count or lineation and usually fewer than seventeen syllables. Poets using either of these forms may or may not attempt one or both of the other conventions of 'traditional' Japanese haiku (a seasonal reference; and some form of disjunction between two elements of the poem, an invitation to the reader to find some intuitive way of bridging it, perhaps inviting an 'internal comparison'.) A few individual poets have ventured a more vernacular form of their own, notable examples being the monostich (single metrical line, actually an alexandrine) developed by the French poet Emmanuel Lochac (1886 -1956) and sometimes employed by other haikuists; the 'little Japanese verses' of Rainer Maria Rilke (1875 -1926) which, though in three lines, may have fewer than 17 or up to 31 syllables; the rhyming haiku of Paul Muldoon; and the quatrain form (he calls it 'haiqua') which has until recently been the staple of Tito's (Stephen Gill's) output.

It will be seen, both from the originals and the translations, that as yet the preference for 'free form' is strongest in the English-speaking countries, though poets in other countries seem to be moving in that direction. In the European context, not feeling bound by the traditional constraints of Japanese haiku generally helps Western poets to make best use of the idioms, rhythms and other resources of their own language, and to be relevant to their own society's needs of poetry. It may result in writing that can more easily be assimilated into indigenous literature and culture. This writing should nonetheless be faithful to the spirit and approach of haiku.

For haiku poets commonly try to express something they may call 'haiku spirit', deriving to a greater or lesser extent according to personal inclination, and directly or indirectly, from some exposure to Eastern poetry and philosophy. One characteristic of this spirit is loving acceptance of the world we live in; thinking of humanity as part of the natural world, not outside it, nor estranged from it. Today's haiku poet is involved with the world of manmade things as well. Occasionally misrepresented as a kind of 'nature poet', he or she is rather an environmental or eco-poet, who tries to represent the intimate interconnections between humanity and nature. Other characteristics of haiku spirit are self-effacement, one aspect of which is to avoid being flamboyantly 'poetic'; keeping haiku open-ended and free of comment and aphorism so as to allow space for readers to add in their own perceptions; faith in intuition rather than intellect; gentle, sometimes wry humour. Whilst brevity, clarity, and directness are the normal hallmarks of haiku (though this doesn't exclude occasional ambiguity), some poets who write in a more obscure, or lush, or loaded style have found a place in this anthology.

This small book appears when politicians and indeed the public in general are agonising over what Europe is and might become, and so it may be timely. Though it isn't the role of poets to break a lance for particular political causes, they tend to think of themselves as being in the van of public opinion, leaders by reason and intuition and emotion; it is in their job description. Many, if not all, will be comfortable with Goethe's description of himself as a citizen of the world. Jingoism and chauvinism are firmly out of fashion in the poetry world. Even though haiku poets have adopted (and adapted) a poetic form from the far side of the globe, this applies to them no less than to other poets.

We hope to have exemplified how one small poetic activity is serving to promote understanding and collaboration, as well as the development of a shared micro-culture, among all European peoples.

David Cobb

EURO - HAIKU

Dimitar Anakiev

Serbia & Montenegro

Пролећно вече:
под точком транспортера
прегажен гуштер.

spring evening — wheels
of a truck carrying troops
crushing a lizard

Anonymous C8th monk

Ireland

rorúad rath;
  rocleth cruth;
ro gab gná
  giugrann guth.

bracken, shapeless,
  has turned red;
the barnacle goose
  raises its head

Jean Antonini   *France*

croa croa aussi croa   caw caw and caw again
dans les poumons du corbeau   also in the crow's lungs
particules de suie   particles of soot

Annie Bachini   *England*

day after day
bits of the chained bicycle
disappear

Robert Bebek   *Croatia*

prekrstivsi se,   I cross myself
vise ne znam sto je znoj   and can't tell holy water
a sto vodica   from my own sweat

Martin Berner   *Germany*

rolltreppauf   up the moving stairs
immer mehr   more and more
Himmel und Wolken   sky and clouds

Ginka Biliarska   *Bulgaria*

циганска любов —
на пътя черга просната
до залеза на лятото

gipsy love
rugs sprawling on the road
till summer ends

Patrick Blanche   *France*

Premier froid d'automne
Le fibroscope lentement
explore un poumon

First chill of autumn
Slowly the fibroscope
explores a lung

Dejan Bogojevic   *Serbia & Montenegro*

ponoc —   midnight —
neonska reklama   a neon advertisement
osveti oci psa   ignites a dog's eyes

Gerd Börner   *Germany*

Die Dörfer im Tal   villages down below
so nah sind sie sich   how close to one another
von hier oben   from up here

Juan Cervera   *Spain*

Sigue habitada
de algo más que silencio
la vieja casa

it continues lived in
by something more than silence
the old house

Henri Chevignard   *France*

deux heures du matin
un tout petit insecte
traverse la page neuf

two in the morning
the tiniest of insects
walks across page nine

Dominique Chipot   *France*

piétinée   trampled
l'herbe devant sa tombe   the grasses before his grave
repousse   rise up again

Carlo Cignetti   *Italy*

Oh il profumo   oh, the perfume
il colore del fumo   the colour of smoke
   il pericolo   the danger

David Cobb   *England*

Culloden Moor
my child is searching
for four-leaf clovers

Ion Codrescu   *Romania*

frunzele cad   falling leaves
copacul îsi arată cuiburile   the tree reveals its nests
unul câte unul   one by one

Tony Conran   *Wales*

A black tree, a flute
and the echo of a flute —
dawn on fresh snow

W H Davies   *Wales*

A rainbow and a cuckoo, Lord!
May never come together again;
May never come
This side the tomb.

Mirsad Denjo *Bosnia-Hercegovina*

pismo iz daleka —
na njivi zaboravljena
leži motika

letter from abroad —
on the field
the deserted hoe

Vladimir Devidé *Croatia*

Ljudi izdišu
maglu. Magla udiše
ljude.

People breathe out
the mist. The mist breathes in
people.

Gilles Fabre

France / Ireland

A perfect bookmark,
if it was longer,
this grey hair of mine.

Kaj Falkman

Sweden

På skaren
över nya året
utbrända raketer

On the frozen crust
of the new year
burnt out rockets

Volker Friebel   *Germany*

Am Hölderlinturm
ein Ruder taucht tief
in den Himmel.

by Hölderlin's tower
a rower sculls deep
into the sky

Georges Friedenkraft   *France*

S'endort en héron
se coule en un lit de plumes
se réveille femme.

fall asleep a heron,
submerge in a feather bed
wake up a woman

Johann Wolfgang von Goethe   *Germany*

Über allen Gipfeln	Above each mountain peak
ist Ruh,	there's peace,
in allen Wipfeln	in every treetop
spürest du	you sense
kaum einen Hauch;	scarcely a breath;
Die Vögelein schweigen im Walde.	the little birds are silent in the woods.
Warte nur, balde	Patience, for soon
ruhest du auch.	you'll be at rest too.

Ioan Gabudean   *Romania*

apune soarele: the sun sets —
pictorul rămăne cu pensula   a painter sits with his brush
după ureche   behind one ear

Carlos Jorge Gomes   *Portugal*

diasem vento   windless day —
ainda mais medonho   even more menacing
o espantal ho   the scarecrow

Caroline Gourlay   *England*

low cloud on the hill
a pheasant separated
from his call

Dag Hammarskjöld   *Sweden*

Pojke i skogen.
Kastanda söndagsstassen
leker han naken.

Boy in the forest.
Throwing off his Sunday best
to play naked.

Jean-Pierre Hanniet   *France*

Ce chapeau qui pleut
de l'ombre sur tes seins blancs:
un désir s'envole

The hat bestows
its shadows on your white breasts:
an urge starts to grow

Hanne Hansen   *Denmark*

Min datters gave
en mellemrød stofrose
til mit hvide hår

my daughter's gift
a soft-red fabric rose
for my white hair

Seamus Heaney   *Ireland*

Dangerous pavements.
But I face the ice this year
with my father's stick.

Claire Bugler Hewitt   *England*

solar eclipse
and at the darkest point
you call my name

Friedrich Hölderlin   *Germany*

... die Mauern stehn
sprachlos und kalt, im Winde
klirren die Fahnen

... the walls stand
speechless and cold, and the flags
bluster in the wind

Clelia Ifrim   *Romania*

Crabii caută
stele căzute-n mare
cerul răvăşit

crabs scramble on
stars falling on the sea —
the sky in their claws

Alain Kervern   *France*

Sous les pas des danseurs   Under the dancers' feet
l'attraction terrestre   the Earth's gravity
exorcisée   exorcised

Marianne Kiauta   *Netherlands*

het zompig moeras   the squelchy swamp
hoe innig het afscheid neemt   how ardent its farewell
van mijn lieslaarzen   to my long waders

Ingrid Kunschke   *Netherlands / Germany*

winteravond —   winter evening —
met kleine steekjes krijgt pop   with tiny stitches dolly
haar glimlach terug   gets back her old smile

Emmanuel Lochac   *France*

Grelottante forêt,   Shivering forest,
    replique de mon coeur.   a replica of my heart.

Willem Lofvers   *Netherlands*

Jupiter verschijnt —   Jupiter appears
dakpannen rammelen   — roof tiles rattle
in de winterwind   in the winter wind

Martin Lucas   *England*

morning mist
a workman whistles
no particular tune

Horst Ludwig

Germany

"Sie sind ja noch jung." —
Ich sag das zum ersten Mal
in meinem Leben.

"But you are still young." —
The first time in my life
I've said those words.

Nikola Madžiron

Macedonia

Zaledenel vodnjak.
Na ledu —
kovanci.

Frozen fountain.
Coins
on the ice.

Giovanni Malito   *Italy*

sul sedile I piedi
nudi nell'aria
russa un marinaio

on the bench
bare feet in the air
a sailor snores

George Marsh   *England*

summer's end nears —
now the slow bee allows
stroking of fur

Andrew Marvell *England*

Annihilating all that's made
To a green thought
In a green shade.

Bart Mesotten *Belgium*

Ik rijd negentig.
In mijn auto zweeft rustig
een wilgenpluisje.

Driving at sixty.
Gently into my car
floats a willow seed.

Paul Muldoon   *Northern Ireland*

The old stag that belled
all night long, tail-end of rut.
How my own heart swelled.

James Norton   *Ireland*

Coughing —
and the stranger upstairs
coughs, too.

Luko Paljetak

Croatia

I dalje nosi
na leđima svoj teret
ubijeni konj.

Still carrying
the load on its back
a lifeless horse.

Rainer Maria Rilke

Germany

Kleine Motten taumeln schauernd
            quer aus dem Buchs;
sie sterben heute Abend und
            werden nie wissen,
daß es nicht Frühling war.

Little moths stagger shuddering
            out of the box-tree;
tonight they will die and never know
it was not yet spring.

Gabriel Rosenstock   *Ireland*

Moillíonn
   an lacha fhiáin ...
      luas na habhann

the wild duck slows
   to the pace
      of the river

Susan Rowley   *England*

in the car   finding
the distance from seat to wheel
is still yours

Sophia Russinova   *Russia*

пуша на балкона   on the balcony
след скарването с теб   smoking
преди половин пакет   after the quarrel
                                                half a pack ago

Edin Saračević   *Slovenia*

prvi dan v EU   our first day
sonce še vedno   in the EU — the sun
vzhaja na vzhodu   still rises east

Zoe Savina   *Greece*

πολλές συμβουλές
μέσα σ' αυτό το βιβλίο
— γυαλιά στον πάγκο

too much advice
in this volume ...
glasses on the bench

Slavica Šavli   *Slovenia*

Še bose ovce
vidijo le hrbet
miline ozvezdij.

even sheep on bare feet
see the galaxies' grace
only from behind

George Seferis

Στάξε οτη λίμνη
μόνο μια στάλα κρασί
και σβήνει ο ήλιος.

Greece

Spill into the lake
but a drop of wine
and the sun vanishes.

Grzegorz Sionkowski

stłuczone lustro —
w każdym kawałku
te same oczy

Poland

broken mirror —
in each piece
the same eyes

Marcel Smets   *Belgium (but in Latin)*

Ad telephonum   On the telephone
obdormivit mulier   a woman dozes off
murmurat imber   the patter of rain

Alan Spence   *Scotland*

mouse-tracks
across the frozen lard
in the frying pan

David Steele   *England*

shipping oars
I hold my breath to hear
snow on the water

Dimitar Stefanov   *Bulgaria*

Птиците, листата ...   the birds, the leaves,
Есента не е ли   autumn — isn't this
да губим нещо?   the time to lose things?

Dietmar Tauchner

Austria

Frühlingsputz ...
die dünne Staubschicht
auf meiner Brille

spring clean —
thin film of dust
on my spectacles

Hubertus Thum

Germany

Irgendwo Tango.
Kröte und Mond
wandern zum Teich

Somewhere a tango.
The moon and a toad
making for the pond.

Tito (Stephen Gill)   *England*

This is the hour
Looked for, strived after —
A stray dog runs noiselessly
Under stars.

(Arashiyama, Kyoto, 11.11.74)

Ewa Tomaszewska   *Poland*

po dwudziestu latach   after twenty years
polerowania lustra   of polishing the mirror
pękanie lodu   breaking the ice

Tomas Tranströmer

Sweden

Rentjur i solglass.
Flugorna syr och syr fast
skuggan vid marken.

Reindeer in sun's glare.
Flies stitch and sew fast
the shade to the ground.

Guy Vanden Broeck

Belgium

Un froid mordant —
irritée, ma langue cherche
la molaire cassée.

biting cold —
my tongue's tic seeking out
the broken molar

Carlo Vasio *Italy*

Pigne sul tavolo
  un tempo è stata viva
    la primavera

pine cones on the table
a brief reawakening
of spring

Zinovy Vayman *Russia*

лепной потолок
адвокаты, мой и её
дружат уже

ornate ceiling
my lawyer, her lawyer
already friends

Max Verhart   *Netherlands*

onder de douche
herinneren mijn blote voeten
mij aan mijn dood

under the shower
my bare feet remind me
I shall die some day

Mirko Vidović   *Croatia*

mladići
rasipaju sjeme po
rovovima

in the trenches
red-blooded young men
shooting their semen

Judit Vihar

Hungary

régi kunyhóban
megmeritem vödrömet
a Mült kütjában

behind an old hut
the well I drink water from
belongs to the past

Florence Vilén

Sweden

Den beska smaken
av fjärde koppen te
i sommarregnet

the bitter taste
of a fourth cup of tea
in the summer rain

Imma von Bodmershof

Austria

Leichthin fährt das Boot,
im sanftgeblähten Segel
unsichtbaren Wind.

the boat moves lightly,
in the gently-blown sail
the wind unseen.

Udo Wenzel

Germany

Sommerwiese —
ich werde Eis
in Deiner Hand

summer meadow —
in your hands
I turn to ice

Klaus-Dieter Wirth   *Germany*

Auf dem Weihnachtsmarkt.   Christmas market.
Engel Stück sieben Euro,   Angels seven euros each,
Ochs und Esel zwölf.   ox and ass are twelve.

William Wordsworth   *England*

  The one blasted tree
and the bleak music
   from that old stone wall.

Alenka Zorman   *Slovenia*

vroč večer   hot evening
njegov dih   his breath
edina sapica   the only air

LINKS

Austria:
email haikugesellschaft@arcor.de

Belgium (Flanders):
Haikoe Centrum Vlaanderen
Brabançonnestraat 90
3000 Leuven
email karel.hellemans@arts.kuleuven.be

Bulgaria:
Bulgarian Haiku Club,
Sofia 1172
Dianabath POB 72
email ginka-biliarska@yahoo.com

Croatia:
Hrvatsko Haiku Društvo
Smerovišće 24
41430 Samobor

Denmark:
Haiku Group of the Danish Society of Authors
email h.hanne@jubii.dk

France:
Association Française de Haiku
email haikuenfrancais@wanadoo.fr
website http://perso.wanadoo.fr.dominique.chipot/afh/indexafh.html

Germany:
Deutsche Haiku Gesellschaft e.V.
email haikugesellschaft@arcor.de

Hungary:
email: jvihar@ludens.elte.hu

Ireland
Haiku Ireland
website info@haikuireland.org

Netherlands:
Haiku Kring Nederland
A Coenenstraat 22
2584 RH Den Haag
email: max@verhart.org

Romania:
Constanţa Haiku Society
email laura-vaceanu@yahoo.com

Serbia and Montenegro:
email draganjr@bankerinter.net

Slovenia:
Haiku Club of Slovenia (Haiku društva Slovenije)
email alenka.zorman@siol.net

Sweden:
Svenska Haiku Sällskapet
email kaj.falkman@foreign.ministry.se

UK:
British Haiku Society
website http://www.britishhaikusociety.org
38 Wayside Avenue
Hornchurch
London RM12 4LL

http://davidcobb.members.beeb.net/index.html

Haiku Scotland
email haiku.scotland@btinternet.com

Also by David Cobb from IRON Press:

The Haiku Hundred (co-editor)

Jumping from Kiyomizu

The IRON Book of British Haiku (co-editor)

The Dead Poets' Cabaret (editor)